Praise for *The P*

"Your story is your secret weapon helps you find common ground. Bu_, _. you don t know how to tell your story, it could cost you profitable relationships, lost sales revenue, and an empty sales pipeline. *The Power of Authority* will help you make the kind of money you deserve and get the results you want by leveraging the power of your story."

Kevin Harrington
Original "Shark" on the hit TV series *Shark Tank*
Inventor of the Infomercial and Pioneer of the *As Seen on TV* brand

"On my podcasts, 95% of my guests have written books, as it simply showcases that they have invested the time and energy to become an expert on their topic. Yet, so many people, me included, perceive barriers to writing a book. I co-host *The Ziglar Show* podcast with Michelle a couple times per month, and her expertise and passion for book writing won me over. Now, my first book is finally in the works! I'll be massively recommending *The Power of Authority* to everyone, from my listeners to friends and family. Let Michelle remove the real and perceived obstacles that so many people have."

Kevin Miller
Host of *The Ziglar Show* and The *True Life Show* podcasts

"If you're looking for ways to stand out from your competition and be the go-to expert, then you must read this book! *The Power of Authority* will show you how to leverage all your hard work, knowledge, and expert skill in such a way as to get the attention of the people you want to help most."

Dina Dwyer-Owens
Brand Ambassador
Neighborly Brands

"*The Power of Authority* provides a blueprint to leverage your expertise, education, and knowledge. By writing a book, you can become the go-to expert in your field. I highly recommend you read this before your competitors do!"

Tom Ziglar
Speaker and CEO of Ziglar Inc

"Michelle Prince has put together a compelling reason why you need to write a book to better establish your brand. She has also given you the specific action steps to complete that process. I believe this book will become one of the best resources a new author could ever possess. Thank you, Michelle, for this excellent work!"

Robert A. Rohm, Ph.D.
Personality Insights, Inc.

"I've seen *The Power of Authority* increase Revenue, Respect & Results over and over in my own life and the lives of many others! Get this book from my good friend, Michelle Prince TODAY!"

Howard Partridge
CEO, Phenomenal Products

"Yes, authority equals influence. That's why highly successful entrepreneurs earn far more income for *who* they are than *what* they do. Success is not about being the *best* at what you do. Success is more about being known as the authority or celebrity expert in your niche, and authoring a book is the absolute best strategy for quickly moving from commodity to authority.

As the author of seven business books, I can attest to this phenomenon. Becoming an author builds both personal and business credibility, gets you more valuable PR, and because authority equals influence, your book also lowers price resistance.

What holds most business owners back from benefitting from these proven results is the sometimes burdensome task of writing and publishing a book while also running a business. Michelle Prince and her amazing "Book Bound" program have helped countless entrepreneurs to finally get their books done. And now, with this amazing book, *The Power of Authority,* you can write your book, too!

The Power of Authority provides an easy to read blueprint on how to write a book that can transform your business and earning power, by moving you from a provider of services to an authority expert.

As an entrepreneur, you likely have piles of to-be-read books on your desk or nightstand. Take my advice and move Michelle's amazing book to the top of the stack. You'll thank me later."

Jim Palmer
The Dream Business Coach
www.GetJimPalmer.com

"As a CEO of a large marketing firm, I experienced *The Power of Authority* in my own business after writing my first book. It really is one of the best ways to stand out from the competition and establish yourself as the expert. I highly recommend you read this book and put into action the shared strategies so you can leverage *The Power of Authority* in your own business."

Joy Gendusa
CEO, PostcardMania

"Michelle Prince is an amazing speaker, author, and coach. She is also a dear friend I met through Tom Ziglar and Howard Partridge. Her book *The Power of Authority - How to Get the Revenue, Respect & Results You Deserve by Authoring a Book* nails it on the head—the importance of establishing yourself as an authority and expert in your field, and leveraging a book for your brand, credibility, and as a business card. Bravo, Michelle, on all you do to help others succeed!"

Kyle Wilson
Founder Jim Rohn International & KyleWilson.com

"If you want to be known as the leading authority in your area of expertise, then you must read this book! *The Power of Authority* will show you step-by-step how to take what you already know and leverage it in such a way to give you incredible results. Don't wait ... read this book!"

David Phelps
CEO, FreedomFounders.com

"I've seen firsthand how Michelle Prince has leveraged *The Power of Authority* in her own life by being an author. She shares a simple roadmap to enable you to get more revenue, respect, and results in your business."

Mark Timm
CEO, Xponential, Inc.,
Entrepreneur, Author, Speaker, Dad, and Husband

"Writing a book is a big deal. Even better is sharing your unique and compelling story. Michelle Prince is the perfect mentor for distilling your message, and simply and systematically getting your book out into the world. Her approach is not just a lucrative book writing process. It's a journey to self-discovery. Michelle is funny and fun and kind and smart and super-organized. I love her! You will, too."

Ellen Rohr
Member/Franchise Operations Manager
Zoom Franchise Company, LLC.

"I was amazed how just being IN a book, and then later having MY own book, separated me from the crowded field of doctors. Then I met Michelle, and she became our tribe's go-to on all things book related. Why? She wrote the book on it, and she teaches it. This book will share with you her passion for becoming that **AUTHORity** with her wit and wisdom. You too will soon become that **AUTHORity**."

Dr. Chandler George
www.GrowthHackingForYourBusiness.com

"If you're looking for ways to stand out from your competition and be the go-to expert, then you must read this book! *The Power of Authority* will show you how to leverage all your hard work, knowledge, and expert skill to get the attention of the people you want to help most."

Jonathan Sprinkles
Founder, The Connection Lab
13-time author, Award-winning Speaker, TV Personality

THE P☢WER OF AUTHORITY

How to Get the
Revenue, Respect & Results
You Deserve by Authoring a Book

MICHELLE PRINCE

TABLE OF CONTENTS

**"Don't wait
for opportunity.
Create it."**

— ANONYMOUS

INTRODUCTION

I never intended to start a business. I never sat down and mapped out a plan to speak, coach, host seminars, and publish books for people. It was not until after I wrote my first book, *Winning in Life Now: How to Break Through to a Happier You*, that all of these opportunities presented themselves, and I discovered firsthand **The Power of Authority**.

Suddenly, I was presented with new opportunities just because I wrote a book. I was the same person the day before I wrote my book and the same person the day after, but all of a sudden, people saw me differently. I began receiving media requests, invitations to speak at conferences, and opportunities to coach individuals wanting to do the same. All because I was the "authority," the expert. All because I wrote a book.

As I was speaking around the country, I would meet people from all walks of life, and there were two questions that kept coming up. First, *"What was it like working for Zig Ziglar?"* I will share more on my story later, but I was privileged to work for Zig

Ziglar right out of college. Even today, I am still honored to help carry on the legacy of Mr. Ziglar as the "Ziglar Brand Ambassador." Again, more on my story later.

The second question was *"How do you write a book?"* People would come up to me at conferences and say, *"I want to write a book. Can you help me?"* And, of course I said *"YES!"*

So it began. Initially, I worked one-on-one with these people, but as more people came to me, I would schedule conference calls and share everything I knew about writing a book, the publishing process, and building an author platform with as many people as possible. As the demand grew, I began devoting more and more time to helping others. I decided to create an event where others could learn what I knew about creating opportunities through writing a book. That was 2010, and I have been doing these conferences several times each year ever since. All these years later, I am even more convinced that writing a book is one of the best ways to stand out from your competition, establish yourself as the expert, and be the leading authority in your niche.

> Writing a book is one of the best ways to stand out from your competition, establish yourself as the expert, and be the leading authority in your niche.

Becoming a Student of Publishing

When I was writing *Winning in Life Now*, I spent a lot of time learning about the publishing process and all the different options available. I knew a couple of traditional publishers from previous contacts, so I considered taking that route. But as I met with them, I learned very quickly that this was not the right approach for me. It would have been nice to have someone take on the work to get my book published, but that came with a price. I learned that they would not only take a big chunk of the royalties from my book sales, but they would also own the rights to *my* work. To top it off, I would be responsible for doing all the marketing to sell my books. I reasoned that if I was doing all the work to *write* the book and I still had to *market* it, then I should be the one to keep all the *rewards* from publishing the book. I knew there had to be a better way, and I was determined to find it.

I became an avid student of publishing. I learned all I could about the writing, publishing, and distribution process. I studied best practices for working with editors, designers, and printers. I also read everything I could on how to market a book and monetize the message. I ultimately made the decision to officially open my own publishing company, Performance Publishing Group, a company dedicated to helping authors get their messages out into the world by doing things a little differently so that the authors keep their rights, their royalties, and ultimately their rewards.

From Author to Authority

This book is called **The Power of Authority** for a reason. You can't spell *authority* without the word *author*, and there is power when you claim your authority by authoring a book. The two go hand in hand. So, if you have ever dreamed of writing a book to tell your story or grow your business, then get ready. I am going to show you the exact process I followed and have taught to thousands of other busy professionals, just like you. With this book, I am going to teach you how to write a book, build your authority, and monetize your message.

I will show you fun and easy ways to find your topic, get your thoughts out of your head and onto paper, and use the tools to navigate the publishing process. I will also share ways to leverage your book to build your brand and create more revenue-producing opportunities. By the end of this book, you will have learned

You can't spell AUTHORITY without AUTHOR.

everything you need to know to bring your book to life and be the leading authority in your field. You really can get all the *"Revenue, Respect & Results You Deserve by Authoring a Book."* The rest of this book will show you how to follow your dream of writing your very own book!

Follow an expert.

— VIRGIL

CHAPTER 1

BE AN AUTHORITY, NOT A COMMODITY

We live in a society saturated with information. Thanks to the internet, you can easily find anything you could ever want to know or learn how to do online. A quick Google search will reveal customized tutorials on everything from the most common of tasks to the eclectic and obscure. Likewise, you can find an abundance of product reviews, "do-it-yourself" clips, "unboxings," and other instructional videos on YouTube. With over 300 hours of video being uploaded to the platform every minute, there is enough content available to keep you distracted and watching for an eternity!

Furthermore, we have the ability to download podcasts, watch webinars, and read free articles from the most prestigious universities, corporate organizations, and influencers in the world. In short, learning has become digitized, and information is now commoditized. So how can entrepreneurs, business owners, and professional service providers—*people whose occupations require specialized skills, education, or training*—compete with the massive commoditization of information online? To answer that question, we need to answer the following questions:

- How can business leaders distinguish themselves from an increasingly competitive workforce?

- What can business owners do to effortlessly attract a pipeline of new prospects on a consistent and regular basis?

- How can business minded people bring in these qualified customers in a systematized and predictable fashion?

The fastest, most effective way for business leaders to stand out from their competition—and overcome the sea of free information online—is to *become the go-to expert and leading authority in their field.*

This is especially true for professionals, such as:

- Physicians
- Lawyers
- Dentists
- Accountants
- Consultants
- Chiropractors
- Financial Advisors
- Speakers
- Real Estate Agents
- Mortgage Lenders
- Business Executives

...and other individuals who are proficient and certified in highly technical matters.

For these types of referral-based businesses, **becoming the leading authority in your field is often the best way to gain new clients or patients and make more sales.**

Authority Equals Influence

Merriam-Webster's online dictionary defines 'authority' as "The power to influence or command thought, opinion, or behavior." I think that is a perfect definition because when you have authority, it means people are willing to listen to you. They value what you have to say, and they perceive you as the go-to expert. That is when you will *really* have the ability to influence others. As a result of your authority, people will actually *want* to listen to what you have to say.

> For today's business owners and professionals, establishing yourself as the leading authority in your industry is a prerequisite for success.

For today's business owners and professionals, establishing yourself as the leading authority in your industry is a prerequisite for success, and it has never been more so. This truly is **the best way to distinguish yourself from the competition.** If you are going to be in business, lead a company, or be an entrepreneur, then you must be seen as the ultimate authority for your niche. But not just any old authority will do. You have to become *THE* authority—the premier expert. There is a difference here. Let's use the example of a dentist or medical provider. Many of these dentists and physicians go through the same schooling. They have the same college degrees and the same professional certifications. Very quickly, they all begin to look the same. I am not saying that they are not *authorities* in their respective fields. It is just that oftentimes, there is no clear distinguishable attribute that separates one dentist or physician from all the others in the eyes of their patients. Instead, what ultimately makes one dentist stand apart from another is how they have *positioned* themselves as an authority in the marketplace. This positioning of authority is the positive light that they have created so that prospects will see them as THE authority. The authority platform they have built for themselves has enabled them to rise above everyone else. That is why it is so important to be seen as the leading authority in your field. You can't just recognize it, though. You also need to know how you can leverage it to grow your business.

Become an Authority by Being an Author

Books have power. A prospect may throw away your business card, but they won't throw away your book. **That is why authoring a book is the very best way to become an authority in your field.** While other mass media channels—like television, podcasts, newspapers, and websites—can provide *exposure*, a book provides exposure *and* immense credibility. Additionally, a book has a much longer shelf life than an article, blog post, podcast, or TV commercial. Just think about it ... books can last years on the bestseller list and, at the same time, be distributed to audiences all around the world through online and traditional retail outlets. Furthermore, very few people ever write a book, so **becoming an author gives you instant credibility and opens more doors for building your business.**

Even though many people think about writing a book, only a small part of the population will actually do it. I once heard a statistic that said only 2-4% of the entire population will ever write a book. Just think about that. There are over 320,000,000 people in the United States alone! This means that since so few people actually become authors, those who do are instantly perceived as being more knowledgeable, valuable, and proficient. As a result, **authors are seen as experts in their fields.** An author is just someone who has taken what they already know—about their profession, passion, or purpose—and put it into a book for others to read. Futurist Herman Kahn once summarized it like this:

> *"Authority is not power; that's coercion. Authority is not knowledge; that's persuasion, or seduction. Authority is simply that the author has the right to make a statement and to be heard."*

When someone writes a book, we instantly perceive them as being more credible and trustworthy. It is a phenomenon that is hard to explain, but it is just that our society perceives that authors must somehow be "better" than everyone else because they went through the time and effort to write a book.

> A prospect may throw away your business card, but they won't throw away your book.

Overcoming the Obstacles of Authoring a Book

Many objections and myths about writing a book are out there, and they can simply intimidate people. That is why so many hopeful authors just never bring themselves to actually write their book. However, like most fears, these obstacles can be overcome with education.

For instance, one common myth is that writing a book is just too hard. People look at authorship and think that it is a huge mountain that is impossible to climb. Or they may begin to experience feelings of insecurity. They might have a poor self-image or lack belief in themselves and their abilities. Another obstacle is that they may feel as though they do not have anything valuable or worthwhile to say in a book. They

> Writing a book is like following a recipe. If you can bake chocolate chip cookies, then you can write a book.

may not think their story is significant, or they may not think they have the expertise or time required to write a book. To some degree, we all fear things we have never done before!

Truthfully, **writing a book is like following a recipe.** I say it all the time ... if you can bake chocolate chip cookies, then you can write a book. It really is that simple!

You can quickly and easily become a published author because it is all about knowing what to do and when. It is about knowing the ingredients to add, the ones to stir, and the right order of steps to follow. The process is even easier when you have an experienced "chef" or in this case, a book publishing partner, to encourage you and walk alongside you in your journey to authorship.

In a future chapter, I will show you how you can effectively tell your story in a way that connects with and inspires others. I will talk about different ways you can efficiently write your book, in little time and without ever having to pick up a pen and paper or sit at a keyboard if you do not want to.

The objections to authorship are far outweighed by the benefits. Especially, if you are a business leader, entrepreneur, or professional service provider. You could gain a considerable amount of new business and **finally get the revenue, respect, and results you deserve with your book.** By implementing a few of the steps that I am going to share with you, you can **position yourself as an expert.** By authoring a book, you can stand above your competition and be recognized as the ultimate leading authority in your field.

Refuse to Be a Commodity and Increase Your Revenue as an Authority

In this **first chapter**, and throughout the rest of this book, I am going to show you how you can instantly reach the top of your field and become the leading authority for your market by authoring a book. Refuse to be seen as just a commodity. Decide to position yourself as an authority, and you will begin to reap the rewards that

> Authoring a book can impact your sales, increase your revenues, and present more opportunities for growing your business.

being an expert brings. I will share multiple ways that authoring a book can impact your sales, increase your revenues, and present more opportunities for growing your business.

In **Chapter Two**, we will discuss specifically why clarity is key to becoming the authority in your field and the consequences of not having it. Then, in **Chapter Three**, we will look at all the ways authoring a book can help you get more revenue, respect, and results in your business, and establish you as THE leading authority in your field. We will look at real life examples of how business owners like you have authored and created more opportunities in their business with new clients, more revenue, and greater leverage.

In **Chapter Four**, I will share how to use the power of your story to instantly connect with your ideal audience and turn those prospects into warm leads. We will cover ways to use your book to create a consistent brand image for your business, and I will show you how to use your book to "celebritize" yourself. In **Chapter Five** you will learn how to leverage your book into a complete media platform for magnetically attracting new clients or patients. We will also go over how a book can create new revenue streams for your business, such as speaking engagements, consulting projects, and coaching assignments.

In **Chapter Six**, we will get down to the nitty-gritty of authoring your book. We will cover how to find your book's topic and tell your story in the most effective way possible. In **Chapter Seven**, we will talk about the publishing process and the different options for bringing your book to life, and we will look at ways to get your book published quickly, without having to write at all. Along the way, I will share success stories of others who have taken their businesses to new heights just by authoring a book. In **Chapter Eight**, we will tie together all the ways that your book will position you as the leading authority in your field and how you can leverage it.

Becoming an Author Has Never Been Faster or Easier Than It Is Today

Writing a book does not have to be a chore, and it does not have to be a long, drawn-out process either. In fact, I regularly see first time authors have their book published within three to six months, and some even sooner. That is the entire process from beginning to end, from the time we get the manuscript to the time that the author gets to hold the finished book in their hands. Obviously, that can go quicker or take a bit longer, depending on the availability of the author. The days of waiting for two years or more just to make it on the printing schedule of a traditional publisher are long gone.

So, if you have ever entertained the idea of writing a book or if you feel you have a story to share with the world, then now is your chance. And if you are a business leader, entrepreneur, or professional service provider who wants to grow your business and establish your position as an authority, then authoring a book is the right step for you. If you are a mid-career professional, in transition, or thinking about the next phase of your legacy, then authoring a book can help you open new doors of opportunity.

Whatever your professional aspirations are, they can be enhanced and expedited with **the expert authority positioning available to you when you author a book.** The rest of *this book* will show you step-by-step how to become a published author. Congratulations on your desire to take this journey with me. Now, let's get started!

"If you want to reach a goal, you must 'see the reaching' in your own mind before you actually arrive at your goal."

— ZIG ZIGLAR

CHAPTER 2

THE POWER OF CLARITY

Once upon a time, an American investment banker stood at the pier of a remote coastal village in Mexico when all of a sudden a small boat with just one fisherman docked. Inside the small boat were several large yellowfin tuna. The American banker complimented the fisherman on the size and quantity of his fish and asked him how long it took to catch them.

The Mexican fisherman replied, *"Only a short while."*

The American then asked, *"Then why didn't you stay out at sea longer to catch more fish?"* The Mexican said that he had already caught enough to support his family's immediate needs and that he was content with what he had.

The American then asked, *"But what do you do with the rest of your day?"*

The Mexican fisherman explained, *"I sleep in late, fish a little, play with my kids, and take siestas with my wife, Maria. Then I'll stroll* into the village during the evening, sip some wine, and play guitar with my amigos ... I have a pretty full and busy life."

The American scoffed. *"I have an MBA from Harvard. I can help you,"* he said rather matter-of-factly. *"You should spend more time fishing, and then with the proceeds, go buy a bigger boat. And with the new profits from the bigger boat, you could go buy several more boats. Eventually you would have a whole fleet of fishing boats, each one manned by their own working crew ... And instead of selling your catch to a middleman, you could sell the fish directly to the processor and open up your own cannery. Then you could control the product, the processing, and the distribution..."* the American paused. *"Of course, you would need to leave this small coastal village and move to Mexico City. Then on to Los Angeles, and after that, on to New York City, where you could run your own angling empire."*

Taken aback, the Mexican fisherman asked, *"But how long will all that take?"*

The American investment banker replied, *"Oh, I don't know. Probably fifteen to twenty years or so."*

"But then what?" asked the Mexican fisherman.

The American banker laughed and said, *"That's the best part. When the time was right, you could announce an IPO, and sell your company stock to the public. You could become very, very rich! You might even make millions!"*

"Millions?! — Then what?"

The American banker answered, *"Then you could retire and move to a small coastal village in Mexico, where you could sleep in late, fish a little, play with your kids, and take siestas with your wife. Then, come evening, you could stroll down to the village where you would sip wine and play guitar with your amigos."*

The Consequences of Not Having Clarity

For the last several years, that cute little story has made its rounds on the internet. And as best as I can tell, it has its origins dating back to 1963 when it was part of a series of stories by German author, Heinrich Theodor Böll. While this is an entertaining tale, it certainly drives home a point worth considering. In all of your working and striving in your career and business, it is important to remember the **reason why** behind all your effort.

In the above parable of the Mexican fisherman, the American investment banker had an endgame goal of relaxing on the beach at the end of his Wall Street career. However, the stress and hassle of the American rat race did not appeal to the slow-paced fisherman, and the banker failed to realize that the embellished destination he described was already available to him in the reality that the fishermen had created for himself. The fisherman could not comprehend spending fifteen to twenty years to create something he already had and that he enjoyed in the present. In short, for the American banker, there was an incongruence

> We may spend our whole life climbing the ladder of success, only to find out when we get to the top that our ladder has been leaning against the wrong wall. — Thomas Merton, the American Monk

between the goals he had described and the reason *why* for his goals in the first place.

Now there are obvious takeaways from both characters' perspectives. For example, it is good to go slow and smell the roses, and contentment can be a virtue. But contentment is not the same as being complacent. If you have big dreams for your life and business, then you will need to set clearly defined goals in order to turn them into a reality. You may have to work hard and work smart to make your dreams come true. That is the kind of thinking that the investment banker had. The only problem was his incongruence. He was lacking a values alignment between his goals and his reason why.

Misdirected ambition is one of the leading causes of frustration and burnout among business professionals today. Thomas Merton, the American monk, once said:

"We may spend our whole life climbing the ladder of success, only to find out when we get to the top that our ladder has been leaning against the wrong wall."

Get really clear on what it is you actually want in your life, and then figure out a way to make it possible through your business.

Some sample questions you can use to help you find clarity include:

- What worked well for you last year that you can capitalize on this year?
- What are your top priorities during this season in life?

- What are your strengths and opportunities?
- What areas could you improve upon?
- What one thing could you do today?

If your *why* is big enough, then you will be able to figure out the *how*.

Clarity on Your "WHY" Is Powerful

Your **WHY** could be your family, your beliefs, your values, your dreams and desires, or your wish to make a better life for yourself and those you love. Maybe your **WHY** is to create more free time for you to enjoy your passions and hobbies, like traveling or other recreational activities that are fun and give your life meaning.

Whatever your **WHY**, you need to make sure that you are completely clear on the goals you have set out to achieve. Make sure that there is a clear values alignment for the *reason* **WHY** behind your ambition. Constantly reflecting on your goals, your progress towards achieving those goals, and the underlining **WHY** behind your goals are essential steps in getting and keeping clarity.

In his best-selling book *Start with Why: How Great Leaders Inspire Everyone to Take Action*, author Simon Sinek states:

"Very few people or companies can clearly articulate WHY they do what they do. When I say WHY, I don't mean to make money. That's a result. By WHY I mean what is your purpose, cause, or

belief? WHY does your company exist? WHY do you get out of bed every morning? And WHY should anyone care?"

This kind of clarity is powerful, and when it comes to goal setting, there are several key areas in both life and business that you should consider. We will talk more about goals and how to set them a little later in this book. For now, I want to make sure that you understand the power that is available to you when you have complete clarity. **Clarity on your why is the key to getting more revenue, respect, and results in every area of life and business.**

> Clarity on your why is the key to getting more revenue, respect and results in every area of life and business.

So, I will ask you again, *"What do you really want?"*

Get Clear on What Success Means for You

Now that you are thinking through what you really want in life, it is time to think through your definition of success. That way you will know what you are working towards, why you are doing it, and how you will know when you get there.

Have you ever stopped and thought through what success means for *you*? Take a moment now to contemplate what your definition of success is.

Success to me is...

_____

_____

_____

_____

_____

If you ask enough people, you will find that success is subjective. Everyone's definition of success is different. For some, success means having more free time. For others, it means having a loving family, and still others equate success to financial gain and material wealth.

People are multi-dimensional, and therefore, success can be a combination of all of these things and more. That is why success is not just about having a business, being great at certain skills, having various certifications, or having a desire to help people.

It is more holistic than that. While all of those areas may be essential ingredients, they are not the *whole* recipe. True success comes when you are able to:

- Get absolutely clear on your why and your core message.
- Leverage your accomplishments in order to help more people.
- Be the real you regardless of the situation you are in, whether it is in a public setting or in private.
- Build your brand and monetize your message so that you are seen as the leading authority in your field.

- Stand out from the crowd and rise above your competitors so that you are positioned as the clear and obvious choice for your customers and prospects.

Success Comes by Being an Expert and a Specialist

After you have begun to think through what you really want in life and how you define success, you are ready for the next step in the clarity process. Begin now by taking some time to consider how writing a book will help you reach these things through your business. Ask yourself, *"What do I really want in my business?"* and *"How will writing a book help me achieve these things?"*

Is it so that you can experience:

- More credibility with prospects?
- Explosive growth in your business?
- The status of being the go-to authority?
- The easy attraction of new opportunities?
- The ability to create multiple streams of revenue?
- A platform for making a difference in the world with your story?

All of these benefits and more are available to you when you write a book. In every field and across every industry, people want to work with the expert. When people have a problem that they need solved, they instinctively want to go to an expert who is a specialist in solving their particular problem.

It really is a simple decision when you stop and think about it. Just picture this. If there was an option for a patient to see a top-rated cardiologist who was well-known and respected in the community or a newly minted M.D. fresh out of college, who do you think most people would choose to see if they needed heart surgery? You would not trust just anyone with a medical degree to perform such a specialized procedure like that, would you?

> **Authoring a book is the fastest way to position yourself as the premier expert for your market.**

Authoring a book can create this same type of specialization and expert positioning for you. Regardless of your industry or business, it is a fact that people trust authors more than they do people in the same profession who have not written a book. **Authoring a book is the fastest way to position yourself as the premier expert for your market.** It lets consumers know that you take your craft seriously and that you are a thought leader in your industry.

Authoring a book gives you instant credibility and creates more opportunities for you. Your book can also serve as a source for creating multiple streams of revenue within your business. And if you have a desire to serve others with your experience or you want to make a difference in the world, you absolutely have to tell your story! Writing a book is the best way to begin sharing your story with the world.

Once you write a book and tell your story, more opportunities will naturally come your way—opportunities for speaking engagements, personal coaching, and hosting events, all of which will allow you to reach more people with your message and increase revenues to your bottom line. But again, it all starts with the power of clarity and getting clear on what it is that you want to *get* out of life, what it is you want to *give* out of life, and *why* you want to do it. Once you have that figured out, you can begin to think about how you can use a book as a vehicle for reaching these goals in your business.

"In the final analysis, you always get paid for your results."

- BRIAN TRACY

CHAPTER 3

MORE REVENUE, RESPECT & RESULTS

In the summer of 1989, I was getting ready to head off to college. As I was preparing to leave, my parents told me that they had a gift for me. They said that this gift was going to "take me places and change my life." Well, in my young adult mind, I kept assuming they were talking about giving me a car. Boy, was I wrong.

My parents did not give me a car. Instead, they gave me a ticket to a seminar, but not just any old seminar. It was a *motivational* seminar. I thought, "I am 18 years old. I don't want to be motivated!" If you have teenagers, maybe you can relate. The seminar was called "Born to Win," and it was hosted by Zig Ziglar. At this point in my life, I had never heard of Zig Ziglar, and I certainly did not want to spend three days with him at this event. I admit that I felt pretty let down when they handed me the conference ticket and *not* the keys to my new ride.

But honestly, in hindsight, I can see how that seminar really was one of the best things that could have ever happened to me. What I heard over those three days was truly life changing, and it set me on the course to finally be able to do what I am doing today.

Face-to-Face With My Destiny

I absorbed everything I could learn from hearing Zig talk that weekend. I took tons of notes and felt that everything he said resonated with me at a gut level. So at the end of the conference, I got in line to have Zig sign my book. As I got closer to him, my enthusiasm grew. And when my turn came next in line, I had one of those moments. In my excitement, I said something to him without really thinking about it. Zig smiled at me and grabbed my book to sign. I looked him straight in the eye and blurted out, "I am going to work for you one day!" I felt so embarrassed. It just came right out of my mouth. But I knew in my gut that it was meant to be.

Well, fast forward five years later. After graduation, I began looking for a job, and the only job I was able to get right out of college was a job selling copiers. That is when life began to come full circle for me. As fate would have it, one day, as I was cold calling on businesses in Carrollton, Texas, I walked up to a building and looked right up at a sign that read "The Zig Ziglar Corporation." I could not believe it! Instantly remembering my proclamation to work for Zig Ziglar, I marched into the building, asked if they were hiring, and as they say, the rest is history.

During my time at Ziglar, I sold books, tapes and CDs, training for corporations, and booked speakers to speak at conferences. Plus, I helped promote dozens of live events. It was then that I really began feeling that one day I, too, would write a book.

I had only worked in the Ziglar corporate office for less than four years when I decided to do something radical. I decided to quit. This was during the early dot.com boom, and I had a shot at making a name for myself in sales. So with that, I entered the technology business, and I spent the next thirteen years selling software in "Corporate America." Even though I was very successful on the outside, I was miserable on the inside. Here I was doing a job that I *could* do, but I did not love. I did not feel fulfilled, and it made me question why I was doing what I was doing. Somewhere in my heart, I just knew that there was more that I was supposed to be doing.

A Whole New World of Opportunities

Deep down I knew that I had always wanted to write a book. I knew that I wanted to make a difference in the world, that I wanted to help people and inspire others, just like Zig had done. But I also knew that I needed to make a good living while doing it. That is when I decided that even though I was not able to leave my corporate job just yet, I would find another way to motivate others. So in 2009, I wrote my first book, *Winning in Life Now: How to Break Through to a Happier You*. I was even able to get the foreword written by Zig Ziglar himself. That was the beginning of a whole new life focused on helping others, but what I did not expect were all the opportunities created just by writing a book.

All of a sudden, because I was an author, people started reaching out to me, left and right. I was invited to speak at conferences, and I began consulting with large corporations, helping their teams to become more productive. I was also invited to appear on all kinds of media outlets, and I became a regular guest on different radio shows and podcasts.

Shortly after writing my first book, I was approached by a woman who asked me to coach her. I told her that I was sorry, that I did not do coaching. After all, I had only written a book. Still, she insisted. I am glad she did because she helped me see another opportunity to use my gifts, and it created another revenue stream for my new business.

> As more people read my book, it was as if they were automatically attracted to me and my message.

Writing my first book opened me up to a whole new world of business opportunities that I did not even know existed, and very quickly I was able to parlay my new book into a rapidly growing business. Not long after that, I wrote my second book, *Busy Being Busy ... But Getting Nothing Done? How to Stop Juggling, Overcome Procrastination and Get More Done in Less Time in Business, Leadership & Life*, endorsed by Brian Tracy, and my momentum just continued to grow.

More Revenue, Respect, and a Reputation for Results

As I look back on it now, it is clear that as a direct result of writing my first book, my business experienced at least three major benefits:

1. More Revenue

My successes really began to compound as a result of writing my book. In *Winning in Life Now*, I shared my journey in personal growth and how I used many of the principles I learned from Zig and others to reach my goals in life. As more people read my book, it was as if they were automatically attracted to me and my message, and best of all, they wanted to do business with me. So my book created an autopilot system for generating new revenue. Just like the lady asking me to coach her, new business opportunities flowed to me on a daily basis. Now I have all types of products, from books, digital courses, and coaching to hosting conferences and running my own publishing company.

2. More Respect

I think my business took off because, ultimately, people began to look at me differently. As an author, I was instantly seen as an authority on my subject, and people always want to do business with an authority. By establishing yourself as the authority, you settle the question in your prospect's mind about your qualifications to help them. When you author

> When you author a book, you instantly become branded as an authority on your subject.

a book, you instantly become branded as an authority on your subject. Your reputation in the marketplace grows, and your new status as an author positions you as a brand to be trusted. When that happens, consumers have more confidence in buying from you as a service provider or business. Perhaps best of all, they feel good about giving you their money.

Consumers want to believe that the service providers they work with are the best in the business. They want them to be the experts at the top of their game. This makes sense because as part of the buying process, people need to be reassured that they are making the best possible decision. They want to know that they are selecting the right solution for their unique needs. As an authority in your field, you can overcome your prospects' fears and objections and thus prevent buyer's remorse from settling in.

Brian Tracy, author of the book *Earn What You Are Really Worth: Maximize Your Income at Any Time in Any Market* says,

"Your reputation is everything ... Any company that can positively influence the way customers think and talk about it to others has accomplished a tremendous feat. It is easier for a company to charge more and sell more in a competitive market when it has an excellent reputation ... It is the same with you. What kind of reputation do you have in your marketplace among the people you know and work with? And what kind of reputation would you like to have in the future?"

As more people found out that I had written a book, I was instantly regarded with more respect. Clients trusted me more, and they gave me more of their time and attention. Having this greater degree of respect gave me a positive reputation in the marketplace, and it elevated my overall status and credibility with new prospects.

3. *More Results*

By authoring my first book, I practically eliminated the need to cold call on prospects. Authoring my book gave me the expert positioning I needed to create a system to almost effortlessly attract new clients at will. Overall, my business experienced much quicker results because of it. Because my respect grew with the popularity of my book, more people found out about how I was helping my clients achieve more for themselves, and the more revenue I was able to bring in because of it.

But Don't Take My Word for It...

Here are some of our publishing clients who have seen similar results in their practices and businesses, simply by writing their book:

"...Writing a book gives you that instant credibility as an expert ... And people are going to want to do business with you just because you wrote the book on the subject. Using Michelle's publishing company was a great experience for me. I went ahead and did the 'Business Card' mini-book, and it's called How to Find an Extraordinary Dentist.

We wrote that book, and we use it as a giveaway at our office just like you would a business card. When patients call and ask questions about our office or about a certain procedure, we get their address and mail them a copy of the book for free. When they read that book, they are going to want to come in to see us. Also, businesses refer patients to us, so we drop off copies of the books. Then, they can have them there to give to anybody who is interested in a dentist. It has been a great source of referral business for us.

> Writing a book gives you that instant credibility as an expert...And people are going to want to do business with you just because you wrote the book on the subject.

Remember, people will toss away a business card, but they will not throw away a book because it has value. People leave it on the counter or on the coffee table, and friends and family come over and see it. They are going to want to look at it, and again, it is just going to help you get more and more business. So this has been great. I love the 'Business Card' mini-book."

— Dr. R. Anthony Matheny D.D.S.,
St. Lucie Center for Cosmetic Dentistry,
and author of *How to Find an Extraordinary Dentist*

"I am so excited to tell you that I have accomplished one of my biggest life goals, working with Michelle Prince and the publishing team. I am so excited to actually have a book done. I know that if I can do it anyone can do it. It is amazing! Even just having a digital version of the book has opened doors for us. It is giving us credibility. That was an amazing thing for my practice and my credibility. I show it to my patients all the time—that I have been in a book, that I have actually written a book. We are now working on our third book with Michelle and her publishing company, and we will likely have many more to follow."

— Dr. Jason West D.C., N.M.D., F.I.A.M.A., D.B.D.C.N.,
West Clinic and author of *Hidden Secrets to Curing Your Chronic Disease* and *Hidden Secrets to Healthy Living*

"Michelle Prince and the publishing team helped me with my full-length book, Miserably Successful No More. That book went on to become an international bestseller and number one on Amazon in its category. Recently, they helped me with a "Business Card" mini-book #UsToo: Bridging the Global Gender Gap. These books have opened doors for me that I had no idea could be opened. This includes lucrative

> These books have opened doors for me that I had no idea could be opened.

international keynotes, two TEDx Talks, standing ovations, global consulting, media interviews and national awards. My original frameworks are being used in 23 countries. Thank you Michelle!'

— Debjani Mukherjee Biswas, founder of Coachieve, LLC, and author of *Miserably Successful No More* and *#UsToo: Bridging the Global Gender Gap*

Over the years, I have helped literally thousands of other professionals experience similar results in their businesses by simply writing their first book. Time and again, I have seen it happen in my own business and in the businesses of the clients I helped become authors. Quite simply, writing a book helps you to:

- Establish yourself as the leading, go-to expert in your field
- Differentiate yourself as the logical, best choice
- Gain more revenue, respect, and results
- Have more leverage in charging fees
- Get instant credibility with prospects
- Stand out from the competition
- Have more opportunities
- Attract more clients

As I helped my clients get the revenue, respect, and results they wanted in their businesses, my reputation continued to grow. As a result, my business grew because of it. I can best explain it with one of my favorite Zig Ziglar quotes: *"You can have everything in life you want, if you will just help enough other people get what they want."*

Going From Success to Significance

Even though I was very successful in software sales, it was not until I wrote my first book and launched my business that I found my true calling, or what my friend Tom Ziglar calls "significance." Tom describes it this way in his new book *Choose to Win*:

> **"Significance is when you help others be, do, or have more than they thought possible." — Tom Ziglar.**

"Significance is when you help others be, do, or have more than they thought possible."

If you are already successful in business, then writing a book can help you leverage that success for even greater success and significance. It can help you create a legacy and give you a platform for serving others. If you are looking to use a book to grow your business, then it can separate you from the competition, give you more opportunities for advancement, and increase the fees you charge as a speaker, consultant, or coach.

After I had written my first book, I was still the same person I had been in my corporate job. Only now, I had a greater belief in myself. I had more passion, faith in my purpose, and clarity for my mission in life. That is when I hit the next level of success and broke into the realm of "significance." But it all started because I had the courage to step out and share my story in a book.

"A brand is the set of expectations, memories, stories, and relationships that, taken together, account for a consumer's decision to choose one product or service over another."

— SETH GODIN

CHAPTER 4

HOW TO BUILD YOUR BRAND AND MONETIZE YOUR MESSAGE

We all want to be successful in our professional lives. We want our businesses to grow and prosper. We want to effortlessly attract new clients. We want to be able to raise our rates and the fees we charge. Perhaps best of all, many of us want to have greater flexibility in how we spend our time. As entrepreneurs, sales professionals, service providers, business executives, coaches, consultants, and speakers, we tend to want to be able to exercise control over our careers, as well as our paychecks and our schedules.

> The one and only reason your business exists is to be a vehicle to help you achieve your life goals.
> — Howard Partridge

In most cases, we want to know that we can spend less time and effort working *in* the business so that we can spend more time working *on* the business ... or just have more time to do whatever it is we love doing outside of work. My friend Howard Partridge says, "The one and only reason your business exists is to be a vehicle to help you achieve your life goals."

We want to know that when we grow in our professional life, our personal lives will also benefit. Many of us want to know that we can make a positive difference in the world through our businesses. Well, I want to tell you that this can be the year that you will finally achieve all these things and more—more clients, more opportunities, higher fees, and greater flexibility with your time. This can be the year that you choose to make all of your professional dreams come true.

In this chapter, I am going to reveal the keys to doing so, by utilizing a few insider secrets of personal branding. And along the way, I will share some practical ways you can share your story, monetize your message, and grow your business to impact the world.

Establish Yourself as THE Leading Authority

What do Dr. Oz, Dave Ramsey, and Brené Brown all have in common? All three of them have built a thriving personal brand-based business, and they have established themselves as the go-to expert in their fields. They have done so by building an authority platform to share their story and monetize their message with multiple streams of revenue. While they all use a variety of media to accomplish these purposes—such as speaking at live events, hosting radio or TV shows, and creating a thriving online presence with social media—from what I can tell, their initial boost of popularity with the mainstream audience came after they wrote a book.

- Dr. Oz wrote his first book, *Healing from the Heart*, in 1999, five years before he was a guest on Oprah.

- Dave Ramsey mentions on his website that he self-published the first version of his book *Financial Peace* in 1992, and then started selling copies of it from the trunk of his car. Not long after that, he and a friend started a local radio call-in show called *The Money Game*, now nationally syndicated as *The Dave Ramsey Show*, and is one of the most influential leaders in money management.

- Dr. Brené Brown is a research professor at the University of Houston where she holds the Huffington - Brené Brown Endowed Chair. She has spent the past two decades studying courage, vulnerability, shame, and empathy. She is the author of five #1 New York Times bestsellers and the star of the new Netflix special, *Brené Brown: The Call to Courage*. Brené shares on her website that she self-published her first book, *Women and Shame* in 2004, and in 2007 Penguin purchased that book and republished it as *I Thought It Was Just Me*. In June 2019, CEO Magazine reports that Brown's 2010 TED Talk, *The Power of Vulnerability*, has been viewed more than 40 million times and is one of the top five TED Talks ever.

In every case, each of these three experts initially wrote a book that helped to establish them as the leading authority in their respective fields. Even though they already had the training, education, and certifications to be successful, their books assisted in building a public platform for sharing their message, and the status of being an author gave their personal brand-based businesses a greater degree of credibility.

People Buy From People

You are the most important part of *your* success. When you let people see you through your brand, they will connect with you and will want to do business with you. That may not sound groundbreaking in its simplicity, but when applied, the implications of this principle are staggering. The saying really is true: *People do business with those they know, like, and trust.* One of the best ways to get people to know you is through the brand you create, just like Dr. Oz, Dave Ramsey, and Brené Brown did.

I know that many times in business, people want to present themselves as professionals. But more often than not, they just come off as being too serious, stoic, or just plain boring. When you share your story in your brand, it allows people to see your personality and style, and it creates opportunities for connection. Yes, you should be professional, however you define that. But do not forget you are also a person, and *people always buy from people.*

> People do business with those they know, like and trust.

Reaching the next level of success for you may be dependent upon your ability to increase your credibility with prospects, or maybe the thing holding you back from greater breakthroughs is finding the right positioning in the marketplace. Maybe the key to commanding higher fees in your business is to establish that element of prestige or cement the perception that you are the established authority in your field. Or maybe you are just really competitive, and you want your competition to run when they see you coming. Whatever it is that drives you, know that with the clarity principles I shared with you in Chapter 2 and the branding principles I am going to share with you now, nothing will be able to stop you from achieving your desired level of success.

> "So what's your message? Can you say it easily? Is it simple, relevant, and repeatable? Can your entire team repeat your company's message in such a way that it is compelling? The essence of branding is to create a simple, relevant message we can repeat over and over so that we 'brand' ourselves into the public consciousness."
>
> — Donald Miller

And, if your next level of success comes when you get intentional about building your brand and then leveraging it so that you can make more money, then let's talk about what a brand is. I mean, really think about this. We buy products and services every single day. All across the world, people buy hundreds of thousands of items from brand name companies, often without much forethought, so there has to be something driving this.

What Is a Brand?

Branding is an ever-present part of our lives, and while we may have an idea of what a brand is, sometimes we get a brand confused with other things. For example, a brand is not a logo, and a brand is not a website. Now those things might be part of it, but those things alone are not the actual substance of a brand.

A brand is more of a feeling. It is the feeling you get from a person or company. It is the feeling you give off to your clients and prospects as well. Your brand is a part of a process that starts when people first meet you. So start by asking yourself if you are giving them the right kind of feeling? Do you make them feel excited and energized, or do you run from you?

A brand is also a perception. It is how prospects perceive you. Do not forget that perception is reality, especially for our clients. How clients and prospects perceive you, how you make them feel, and how they experience you are all components of your brand. Of course, you can tie all that in with the marketing elements of a website and logo. But your website and your logo, and anything else, should be used to communicate the experience you want to give—the feeling of your brand.

Ultimately, my favorite definition of a brand is that it is a promise. Your brand is the promise you make to your prospects, your clients, and the people you meet every day, whether online or off. Your brand is the promise you make that says you are going to do something for them—solve their problems, meet their needs, or satisfy their wants and desires. So when you think about your brand, consider the promises you

> Your brand is the promise you make to your prospects, your clients, and the people you meet every day.

are making to your prospects, as well as the feelings, perceptions, and experiences you want to provide them.

Promise and Perception

Often when I am speaking from the stage, I will ask audiences to shout out the brand names of companies I describe, just by sharing their promises. For instance, I will say, *"You could save 15% or more on your car insurance...,"* and the audience will shout out "GEICO." Or *"When you're here, you're family,"* and people will shout "Olive Garden." We remember these famous brands and others like them because they have been so good at constantly delivering on their promises and reinforcing their brand with their messaging.

It is the same with your brand promise. You need a short, succinct way of describing the benefit you provide to clients. Whether you realize it or not, you are communicating your brand promise every single time you see or talk to somebody. When you meet them one-on-one or at a networking event, the brand promise you communicate is coming to life for them in real time. Trust me, they will start thinking about you and your brand, and they will begin forming a perception of you, consciously or not. So it is important to be aware of how you are perceived and the brand promise you are making.

3 Steps to Better Branding

Here's the thing ... your brand is how you show up. It is just who you are. So ask yourself, are you being authentic? Are you consistently showing up in the way you want your brand to be perceived? At the end of the day, your brand is ultimately up to you, no matter what.

In the rest of this chapter, I am going to show you three easy ways to immediately start branding yourself better, and these are not particularly difficult. They do not require any significant work beyond what you are probably already doing. These tips will help keep you more intentional about building your brand, and they will provide effective ways for you to monetize your message.

1. Identify Your Message

The first step is to identify your message. Your message is very important. I have already told you that your brand is your promise or what you are already communicating. That is why you have to have clarity about what you are providing to your customers. Think about what it is you tell people when asked, *"What do you do?"*

Sometimes this is called the "elevator pitch" or "cocktail answer"—the answer you give to someone at a cocktail party or networking event. It is all about identifying your message. These statements can come off as vague generalizations or throwaway answers, but you should have a thoughtful answer ready anytime you speak with someone.

Essentially, your message can be considered part of your USP or Unique Selling Proposition. Sometimes it is called a UVP, Unique Value Proposition. In professional branding, I like to call it a USP

> **Your Unique Selling / Value Promise tells the marketplace who it is you serve and what kind of benefit you give them.**

or UVP, but the "P" in this case stands for *promise*. Your "Unique Selling / Value Promise" tells the marketplace *who* it is you serve and *what* kind of benefit you give them. To help you think through this statement, I encourage you to write down the answers to these basic questions:

- *Who do you want to help?*

_____

_____

_____

_____

- *Why do you want to help them?*

_____

_____

_____

_____

- *Specifically, how do you help your customers/patients?*

_____

_____

_____

_____

Never let a prospect question why you are the one they should work with.

If you do not have a solid answer to these questions, then I encourage you to make time this week to think through them. If you already have a clear answer to each question, then that is great. Maybe you are an attorney specializing in elder law or a financial advisor who specializes in retirement planning. Perhaps you are a leadership coach serving CEOs in transition. Whatever it is you do; you have to have clarity about *who* it is you help and *why* you do it.

Remember that no one really cares about *what* you do. They only care about *how* what you do can serve them. In business, we are all just serving each other anyway. We get rewarded for our services with those little green pieces of paper, but at the end of the day, we are really just serving others. We should serve them well. So let your prospects know how you can serve them.

Next, your message should tell them why they should listen to you. This can be a hard question to answer, but you have to be ready to explain why you are the best choice at what you do. This could be because of your experiences, your passions, your skills, and your education. Either way, it is important you let people know why they should listen to you. Let them see your abilities through your brand promise, and never let a prospect question why you are the one that they should work with.

Make Your Message a Mission

Another way to think about your message is to describe it as a "mission." That may be a different or new way for you to think about it, but it could be the key to your breakthrough. To say that you are on a mission is aspirational. It inspires people. It piques their curiosity. It will attract the right prospects and make them want to join you.

Instead of saying *"Oh, I own a business"* or *"Oh, I am a physician/ lawyer/ accountant/ financial planner/ coach,"* think of how much more impactful it sounds if you say, *"I am on a mission to help seniors reduce their liabilities and create more effective ways of estate planning."* Or you could say, *"I am on a mission to help senior executives transition into the next phase of their lives and find fulfillment in retirement."* Whatever you do, you can create more meaning by turning your message into a mission, and your mission into a movement.

Do not just say you are in business. Instead, be on a mission with everything you do. People want to be involved in something bigger than themselves. They want their lives to matter, and missions definitely matter. A mission points to a movement, and movements are contagious. When somebody is on a mission that you resonate with, doesn't their excitement just make you want to be a part of it? If your message—your mission and your movement—is presented to the right audience at the right time, then your prospects will naturally want to be a part of it.

> A mission points to a movement, and movements are contagious.

2. Tell Your Story

Everyone has a story. I do not have to spend five minutes with you to find out that you have a story and your clients want to hear it. People want to know why you do what you do, why you are so passionate about oral health or helping people find their dream home. They want to know why you care and why they should care, too. Believe it or not, people can learn from your story, and your expertise will make an impact in other people's lives. Your story matters. It can inspire, educate, and benefit others if you share it. Prospects will connect to you through your story, and that is what people want. We want to connect with others. We want to know that those we interact with on a professional level are human beings just like us. We want to know that they are real, and the best way to do that is by telling your story.

I have said it before, but it is worth repeating: people do business with those they know, like, and trust. It has always been that way. Think about the last major purchase you made. You probably had plenty of options to choose from. Maybe it was a car, or a home, or a piece of jewelry. When you went shopping, you probably had several willing car salesmen, real estate agents, or jewelers that you could have gone to, but you probably ended up buying your item from the person that you connected with and built the deepest amount of trust in, and in the fastest amount of time. So "know, like, and trust" is critical for anyone in business. I believe that the easiest and most authentic way for your clients and prospects to trust you is to know your story. It is that simple.

So what's your story? What can you share with someone, personally or professionally, that would make an impact on them? Maybe your story could explain how CEOs can get more organized, or how entrepreneurs

> **The easiest and most authentic way for your clients and prospects to trust you is to know your story.**

can become more profitable in their businesses. Maybe you have particular insight into your industry, or you have specialized knowledge that can help prospects.

If you are a physician, your story could be added to a collection of your patients' stories, and they can be highlighted in a book. You could compile their cases as a before and after comparison. In this example, your story would intersect with theirs, showing the relief you have provided them through your care and service. The same template could be used for lawyers, accountants, or coaches. Whatever it is, you have a story, and your story is a key part of building your brand.

3. Establish Yourself as the Expert

Finally, number three: Establish yourself as the expert. You can do this in a couple of different ways, but I am going to give you three simple ways that you can take action right away, and immediately see a positive impact to your brand and your business.

Consistent Branding

You need to be consistent with your website, your brochures, your business cards, and letterhead. If somebody finds you on social media or through your website, you need to make sure that all of your messaging—from your story and design to sales copy, logos, photos, and your unique value promise—matches. This is called establishing a brand standard. Basically, it creates a brand "style guide" that helps you know that your professional image is being communicated correctly and that your public perception stays "on brand."

If people have to guess what you do or how you can help them, consider them confused. Sometimes I see business professionals who have one image on their LinkedIn account and another on their website. They might have different logos on their letterhead or outdated copy, and all of that is confusing to people. Confused people do not buy things. They do not give you money. You need to stay consistent to give the perception that you are bigger than you may actually be. This is a very powerful action.

Social Proof

This is more important than you may think, and I do not mean just social media. That is important to an extent, but I am referring to the use of testimonials and endorsements. People like to see that others already trust you, that you have done a good job helping others, and that others have given you money to solve their problems. Prospects want to see tons of blurbs, complete with names and pictures if possible, of all the happy and satisfied customers you have helped. Video testimonials are even better than static text because prospects will know that your endorsements are real.

You can post these video testimonials on your website, on social media, and in your marketing material. They will make your sales messaging more believable. By showing that others have trusted you, prospects will trust you. It creates a kind of economic peer pressure for prospects, in the positive sense of the word.

It is one thing to say, *"Look how great I am in my business,"* but it is a complete other thing when somebody else says it. It is definitely better when others toot your horn. You can take those testimonials and leverage them to gain more celebrity and notoriety in your industry and with prospects. Make sure, however, that you always get a signed release from clients to use their names, faces, words or videos, and then include these testimonials on your website. By the way, your website does not have to be fancy. It is just a part of the social proof process, and it reinforces your mission. Your website should highlight these testimonials and show prospects how you can serve them.

Write a Book

When given the option, people always want to work with the expert authority over the general commodity. When you write a book, people see you as "THE Expert." Your book will give you that instant credibility in your prospects' minds. They will perceive you as being more knowledgeable, more valuable, and better equipped to meet their needs.

> When you write a book, people see you as "THE Expert."

Prospects do not even have to read your book before they start giving you that extra credibility. It is just the way it works. For whatever reason, people perceive authors differently. Authors are seen as special, rare, and often times, as celebrities. As such, being an author brings you more opportunities and greater leverage for your business. Becoming an author is the ultimate key to personal branding.

If you really want to take your business to the next level, you need to build a brand, and a book will help you do just that. Your book will allow you to charge higher fees, and it will open doors for you to speak on stages, or at events and conferences, if you so desire. Of course, your book brings in a great deal extra through the multiple streams of revenue you can spin off of it. That is how you really begin to monetize your message.

"A platform is the thing you have to stand on to get heard. It's your stage. But unlike a stage in the theater, today's platform is not built of wood or concrete or perched on a grassy hill. Today's platform is built of people. Contacts. Connections. Followers. Your platform is the means by which you connect with your existing and potential fans."

— Michael Hyatt

CHAPTER 5

HOW TO BUILD AND LEVERAGE AN AUTHOR PLATFORM

Now that you have clarity about your message and you have a possible topic for your book in mind, it is time to start discussing how you can build your author platform. Remember, people will throw away a business card, but they will not throw away a book. Likewise, when you build an authentic, attractive, and engaging platform, your prospects will be more inclined to follow you and interact with your material. This again will accelerate the "know, like, and trust" process, and it will lead prospects to want to do business with you. An author platform is important because it allows you the opportunity to spread your message even further than a book can.

> An author platform is important because it allows you the opportunity to spread your message even further than a book can.

It creates opportunities for building brand awareness, gaining exposure on multiple media outlets, and attracting a following of interested and qualified customers to your business. This means that you will be better positioned in the marketplace. You will benefit from being omnipresent. Plus, an author platform can give you the tangible benefit of creating additional revenue streams for your business.

When I wrote my first book, I did not necessarily intend to start a business. I wish I had a great story about how I brilliantly crafted a successful business plan, but I am embarrassed to say that I did not have a plan. I did not have a strategy. I did not know how to start a business. All I wanted to do was put my thoughts down on paper and share them with the world. But because I built an author platform, more and more business opportunities came my way. These new revenue streams immediately started to grow my business at a very quick pace, and they allowed me to leave my corporate job in software sales.

You too can benefit from the same platform building strategies I used to promote my book and grow my business. It has never been easier or more cost effective for you to use mass targeted media to leverage your author platform and engage your audience.

Multi-Media for Multiple Learning Styles

I am going to share several platform building strategies that utilize a multi-media approach to marketing. With the endless combinations of online and offline strategies available to you, I want to caution you not to feel overwhelmed with options. Do not feel as though you need to implement all of these strategies. Just find out what works for you. You can begin by testing media that you have experience in, or that you have a natural interest in. Then see if that media channel reaches your ideal prospects, and if it does not, feel free to abandon those efforts and try another option.

There are two reasons that you want to incorporate a multi-media platform building strategy.

1. *You want to create an omnipresent positioning for your ideal prospects.*

You do not have to be everywhere, but you should be front and center on the platforms and channels that your target market engages with. For instance, if you are an elder care lawyer marketing primarily to boomers and seniors, then you could probably skip the Instagram stories. Instead, you might find that advertising with an association or in a publication geared toward seniors is a better fit for your demographic.

If you are in a rural location with a poor or slow internet connection, it might be more valuable for you to host a book signing at your local library. Again, the point is to find what works best for you and for your audience.

2. *You want to appeal to multiple learning styles.*

Your platform is the combined media outlets you use to extend the reach of your book and to grow your business. People learn in different ways. Some people learn by reading. Others learn by watching a video or listening to a podcast. Some prefer one-on-one coaching, and others prefer live events. As you can see, if you present your book material or business solution in one way, then you might miss out on connecting with prospects that have different learning styles.

There are many ways people can absorb your information, so it is good to build your platform across multiple media channels and across multiple learning styles to ensure you are engaging with the greatest number of people who may be interested in your message. We will discuss specific online and offline author platform building strategies that you can incorporate later in this chapter, but the best way to do this is to repurpose the core content of your book in order for it to be used in multiple formats. This will allow you to reach specific segments of your intended audience and connect with them in a way that they naturally learn and communicate. That is the point of building an author platform.

The Communications Revolution

While there are a number of viable offline strategies at your disposal, the sheer convenience and scalability of online communications is undeniable. We live in an online world. Bestselling author, blogger, and marketing consultant, David Meerman Scott, says that we are living through "the most important communications revolution in human history." In his book, *The New Rules of Marketing & PR*, Scott states:

"Johannes Gutenberg's invention of printing with mechanical movable type (circa 1493) was the second most important communications breakthrough in history ... Some 556 years later, in 1995, an even more important communications revolution began ... It was the year that Netscape went public on the success of the

> ## "All the world's a stage."
> ## — William Shakespeare

Netscape Navigator, the first popular product to allow easy inter-net connection and web browsing ... The first 20 years or so were fast-paced, and things changed very quickly. Usage went from a few million people online to billions. But many organizations still aren't communicating in real time on the web" (pg. 28-29).

Today, online communications such as blogs, podcasts, and video streaming services have opened the doors of possibility. With them, everyday entrepreneurs and business owners now have the means of connecting with their target audience in real time. Again, Scott writes:

"Real time means that news breaks over minutes, not days. It's when people watch what's happening on social networks ... and cleverly insert themselves into stories ... The idea of real time—of creating marketing or public relations initiatives as well as responding to customers right now, while the moment is ripe—delivers a tremendous competitive advantage. You have got to operate quickly to succeed in this world" (pg. 136).

So unlike in years past when it was outrageously expensive to run an ad in the *Wall Street Journal* or produce a TV commercial, there is now an abundance of alternative ways you can reach those same audiences at a fraction of the cost thanks to the internet.

Building an Online Platform

This is by no means an exhaustive list of possible online platforms. It is, however, a short list of potential channels in which you might find success. Additionally, because technology changes so quickly, it is important to note that a marketing channel listed here today may be antiquated by tomorrow. So use discernment in exploring these avenues and be sure to test small first. If a media channel proves profitable, then you can always extend your ad spend and scale your results.

Along with each suggested channel, I have listed a short description of how you might use it to promote your book and grow your business.

Ebooks – Reformat your book for Kindle, Nook, or as a free PDF that your website visitors can download in exchange for their email addresses.

Audiobook – Record yourself reading your book, or hire a voice actor, and promote it on Audible or other audio programs. You could even offer it as a downloadable audio file on your website.

Blogs – Start your own blog or contribute a guest post to your industry's top blogs and websites. Your post could even be an excerpt from your book with a directive at the end that guides readers to call your office for more information.

Social Media – Create an author page or business page on sites like Facebook, Twitter, Instagram, and LinkedIn. Be authentic in your posts and share interesting news or relevant updates. On social media, the key is authentic engagement, so be sure to regularly interact with your followers.

Search Engine Marketing – Promote your book through sites like Google, Bing, and YouTube.

Search Engine Optimization – Optimize the meta-themes on your website and embed keywords into all of your blogs so that web searchers can find you faster.

Press Releases – Submit news stories and company updates to local news outlets to feature in their online publications.

Podcasts – Start your own podcast and share it through iTunes, Spotify, Podbean, or Stitcher. If you do not want to start your own podcast, you can be featured as an interview guest on popular shows that may reach your demographic. Do not worry about buying fancy recording equipment just yet. In most cases, all the technology you need to produce and edit high-quality audio and video recordings can be found in your smart phone.

Video – Use YouTube, Vimeo, and other video sharing sites to host and promote short videos that you can share with your audience. You could teach from a section of your book or just highlight client success stories.

Digital Course – Create a course based on the content of your book, and sell it on your website or through sites like Kajabi, Udemy, or Lynda.com.

Email Marketing – Provide a "Contact us" form on your website or collect client emails when they buy your book or ask for more information. Then utilize an email service provider such as Infusionsoft, Mail Chimp, Constant Contact, or Aweber to stay in regular contact with your email list.

SMS Text Messages – Encourage clients and prospects to opt into receiving regular text message updates and relevant offers from you, sent straight to their cell phones.

Webinars – These can be live or pre-recorded, and can be shown automatically on your website, scheduled as an event, or used as a free bonus when someone buys your book. You can elaborate on the content from your book or share an extended cut version of additional, relevant material.

Newsletters – This strategy can be executed either online, offline, or both. It basically entails creating a monthly or quarterly newsletter for your clients. You can highlight relevant news articles that your readers will find helpful and share updates from your office, as well as your industry.

This list is just the tip of the iceberg. There is an abundance of platform building media channels available to you online. So again, just be sure to try different formats and see what best engages your target audience.

Tools for an Offline Platform

While many of the tools in today's business marketing toolbox exist online, it is important to not forget offline strategies as well. Doing so may result in missing an untold amount of new business and unclaimed revenue. Here are just a few of the offline platform building strategies you may find helpful:

Live Events – You could do a live seminar, workshop, or speak at a conference or lunch and learn. Live events are powerful connecting opportunities because they allow you to connect face-to-face with individuals and group members of your audience. If you are giving a keynote speech, then the authority and credibility you have as an author will be amplified. When hiring a service provider, many people desire a personal meeting to establish trust and to explain their needs. If you are a physician, lawyer, accountant, or financial advisor, hosting regular live events may present a great opportunity for you to gain new business.

Referrals – You can gift your book to past clients or patients and encourage them to give you a referral if they were satisfied with your service. Better yet, gift them two copies of your book so that they can pass along the extra copy to the one they referred.

Direct mail – You can do a direct mail campaign to a specific geographic region in your town. You can target households that are most likely inhabited by your ideal clients. You could also use a composite list of consumers based on specific demographics, psychographics, and purchase history.

Print ads – You can promote your book and service through traditional print ads in magazines, newspapers, and shopping mall inserts.

Postcards – Feature the cover of your book and a picture of yourself on the front of a postcard. Then mail it to a targeted list. On the back, create a series of bullet points, outlining how you help prospects. Invite recipients to call your office to schedule their free consultation.

Brochures – Showcase your author status on the front of all your company brochures and pass them out to prospects, at community events, and industry gatherings.

Trade shows – Attend the trade shows that your prospects are most likely to attend, and consider becoming an exhibitor. For example, if you are a tax planning professional, attend a conference or trade show for business professionals. Get set up with a booth and proudly display your book on the table, along with your company brochure and other items. As you have conversations with attendees, gift them a copy of your book and encourage them to set up an appointment with your office if they have any more questions.

Radio – Your book will establish you as an expert in your field. Radio stations are always looking for new experts to highlight for consumer awareness interviews. Contact your local radio station and let them know you are available for interviews. You may also consider running an advertisement on air during a certain program relevant to your audience.

Teleseminars – During your book launch, schedule a live teleseminar to take place before your book is released. Offer a pre-purchase special for people to buy your book in advance, and in exchange, give them an opportunity to interact with you in a private teleseminar.

TV – If you have the resources and it makes sense for your market, consider running a TV commercial during prime time viewing hours. You can also be an interview guest on your local morning news program.

Joint Ventures/Affiliates – Gift copies of your book to complementary and non-competing service providers. For instance, if you are a lawyer, consider partnering with a physician, accountant, or financial professional. When these other service providers come across a likely prospect for you in their own businesses, they can gift them a copy of your book and refer that prospect to you. In exchange, you can pay your referral partner a finder's fee. Be sure to check into the compliance and regulation standards of your industry, first. And always reciprocate the referrals when you can.

Coaching or Consulting – Many larger corporations have HR departments that promote continuous learning, training, and development. These organizations will often hire speakers and outside consultants to come in and train their staffs on a topic such as productivity, sales, or handling conflicts. If your book or business relates to an activity that an organization may be interested in, you can contact the HR manager and send them a complimentary copy of your book. If you let them know you are also available for speaking and consulting, they may hire you to come in and talk to their group. Individuals may also be interested in hiring you as a coach. You will find that many people will resonate with your message, and will want to "go deeper" with you.

Multiple Streams of Revenue

Many of these marketing and platform building channels, such as speaking at live events, consulting, and offering a digital course, can create additional revenue streams for your business. Others like social media, podcasting, and webinars can give you extra exposure to your market and bring in new business, thus indirectly adding to your bottom line. In either case, each of these platform building strategies can do much to highlight your expert authority, promote your book, and help you grow your business.

If you are already utilizing some of these tools, you are on the right track! But maybe you need to stretch yourself a little. For example, if you prefer to do one-on-one coaching, consider taking on some larger speaking requests. Or if you have a physical book now, consider turning it into a digital course or podcast series. I am telling you; it works. I built my own business by following this exact model. Basically, you take the same core content from your book and begin to share it with your audience in a more engaging way.

If I can do this, you can do this, too. It does not take that long either. You have already done the hardest part. That is, you have already accumulated your knowledge and experience. You have a passion, expertise, or business topic that can help people.

> **Take the same core content from your book and begin to share it with your audience in a more engaging way.**

Now you have to take that knowledge and put it out there. You can format it in the best possible way to connect with the most people and appeal to different learning styles in the process. It really is that simple.

"If there is a
book you want
to read but it
isn't written
yet, write it."

— SHEL SILVERSTEIN

CHAPTER 6

HOW TO WRITE YOUR BOOK

Many people think that writing a book is a huge obstacle, or they look at it like an intimidating mountain to climb. The reality is that it is actually very simple, *if* you have a proven process. I am going to share that process with you in this chapter. As I have told you before, if I can do this, you can do this. In fact, if you can cook spaghetti, then you can become an author. You can easily write your book because the process is similar to following any other recipe. All it takes is a few simple steps.

First, you need to know the "ingredients" and make sure you put them in the right order. By following this recipe, anyone can become an author by getting their own ingredients—their topic or story—out of their head and onto paper.

I have an author workshop that I have been doing since 2010 called, "Book Bound" (www.BookBoundWorkshop.com). I host this workshop multiple times per year and in different locations. Since starting this, thousands of aspiring authors have come to get their books out of their head and onto paper. I teach them about the options they have for writing their book, the publishing process, and most importantly, how they can market their book and build their author platform. I also share with them the three main rules of writing, which I will share with you now.

The Three Rules of Writing

As you begin writing your book, it is important for you follow some simple yet important rules to ensure your success as an author.

Rule #1 – DO NOT write a book to make money

Now, I know you are probably thinking, *"Wait a minute. You are telling me that by writing a book, I am going to get more revenue, more results, and more respect. But now you are telling me not to do it for the money?"* Well, here is what I am saying: Do not write a book just to make money on book

> Writing a book is a recipe.

sales. Instead, write a book so that opportunities open up for you as a result. It is from those opportunities that come to you as an author and authority on your subject that you can make more money. You write a book to get more creditability, to become the authority. You write a book to use it as your business card and to build a platform. But do not *just* set out to write a book and plan on getting rich by selling it. If that is the only reason you are doing it, then you might want to reconsider.

Let's do the math. For simplicity sakes, let's say you want to make $100,000 a year. Now take a $20 book and divide $100,000 by 20 and you get 5,000. That is how many books you would have to sell to make that kind of an income. But actually, it is worse than that because you are not going to make $20 per book. There is a cost associated with production and distribution. Let's say your profit on a book is $10. Now when you do the math, you need to sell 10,000 books, which is twice as many books just to hit your goal. So writing a book just to sell it is not the strategy we are talking about. You have to see authoring a book as a way to build your authority and open up opportunities. That is rule number one.

Rule # 2 – DO write a book that combines your passion and experience

Passion and experience are the two essential ingredients in finding your book topic. It can't be one or the other; it has to be both. Think of it this way. If you write a book about something that you love or you are passionate about, but you have never actually done it or you do not have much experience in that area, there is not going to be

> The perfect book is one that comes from the intersection of your passions and your experiences.

any credibility associated with the book. On the flip side, if you write a book about something that you have experience in but no desire or passion for, you may never finish the work needed to complete it because there is no underlying motivation. In this case, it becomes a difficult and uphill battle to get that book written.

The perfect book is one that comes from the intersection of your passions and your experiences. As a business owner, you likely love what you do. That is why you got into it, right? But now take that passion, combine it with your experience and add the fact that you have so much success behind you, and that is where the credibility factor comes into play. Maybe you have a special degree, or you have an industry certification, or you have some outstanding

> "Either write something worth reading or do something worth writing."
> —— Benjamin Franklin

client or patient testimonies that you want to share. Those are the things that showcase your experience.

When you mesh the two, it becomes a book that you want to write and a book that people want to read. So, as you start out to craft your book topic, be sure to remember rule number two: find a subject where you have both passion and experience, and make sure there is a connection between the two.

Finding Your Topic

There is no limit to the potential topics you *could write* about, but the trick is figuring out the right topic for you and your audience. You have to write a book that will benefit the reader, as well as a book you want to write. Otherwise, your chances of failure are very high.

I want to share a formula with you that is guaranteed to help you find the topic for your first book. If done correctly, you should have topics for multiple books.

Go to www.ThePowerofAuthority.com/Topic to download your free "Finding Your Topic" worksheet, or you can grab a sheet of paper and draw a T-chart. At the top, on the left-hand side of your T-chart, write the word 'Passions.' List everything that you enjoy doing or are passionate about. This could be as it relates to your business, but it could be something totally different, something personal. Maybe you love to travel. Do you love to cook? Do you love to manage people or motivate others? Do you love personal development? Do you love leadership? What are some things that you are passionate about? For this exercise, the key to getting the best results is to identify all your passions. Write as many of your passions down as possible.

On the right side of the T-chart, write the word 'Experiences' at the top. List all of your experiences in life, both personal and professional. These could be things that you experienced through your career, through your profession, or through your business. Of course, those are all very important experiences. But consider what else you have experience in. Do you have experience being a father or mother? Do you have experience traveling? Or in real estate? What have been your most meaningful experiences throughout your life?

Now, experience can be tricky because not everything we have experienced in life is positive. Many of our experiences took us by surprise, and we did not want those experiences. But in order to get the full benefit of this exercise, it is important to list as many of these experiences as possible. Maybe you failed in business. Maybe you dealt with bankruptcy or had another personal issue that was painful. Maybe you were able to learn some lessons along the way that could help someone who is in that same situation now.

So when you are looking at your experiences, do not hesitate to list something. Do not limit yourself. Nobody else is going to see what you put on your list. The more you write down, the more you are going to have clarity as to who you are as a person. After all, your story is your story, no matter what you write. You cannot change your story, but you can decide how you want to leverage your story and use your passions and experiences to either help yourself or help others. That is why this exercise clarifies what the heart of your book should be about.

> You can't change your story, but you can decide how you want to leverage your story.

An Example from My Life

To give you a better idea of how this works, I will share a few of my passions. I love the beach. It is a place where I am totally at peace. I connect with the ocean in a way I can't even explain. So, the beach is the first thing on my list. I am also passionate about personal development and growth. I strive to be the BEST I can be. I thoroughly enjoy reading motivational books, attending seminars, and being around other like-minded people who want more for their lives.

I love PUGS! I have two Pugs, Rex and Zoe. Rex is a fun but mischievous little guy, and Zoe is my sweet baby girl. They both provide hours of entertainment in our house, and I can't imagine our lives without them. I am obsessed with Pugs because, well, they really are the most awesome dogs in the world. Right?

I am passionate about making a difference and encouraging others to be their best. You get the idea.

A few of my experiences include working in sales, being a mom, dancing in my younger years, working for Zig Ziglar, and writing a book.

PASSION	EXPERIENCE
Personal Development	Sales
Beach	Mom
Babies	Worked for Zig Ziglar
Like-minded people/Seminars	Dancer
Pugs	Author/Speaker
Faith	Leadership Roles
Making a Difference	Moved a lot as a Child

After you have listed as many passions and experiences as possible, the fun part of this exercise comes when you find some possible connections from one side of the chart to the other. For example, one of my passions is personal development, and one of my experiences is working for Zig Ziglar. Do you see the connection? I am passionate about personal development and being my best self. PLUS I have worked for the MASTER of personal development and have experience applying his strategies to my own life. A natural book topic would be a book about my experiences using the strategies I learned from Zig Ziglar, describing the ups and downs of life and sharing those experiences with the reader.

In my first book, *Winning in Life Now*, which later became an Amazon best seller in two categories, I did exactly that! Not to mention, the book was incredibly easy to write. It literally FLEW OUT OF ME and onto paper in under three weeks. No kidding!

This formula is exactly how thousands of other authors discovered their book topic, and by using it, you will, too.

Now It Is Your Turn

Now it is your turn to give it a try. Look at both of your lists, and see where you can find a connection, a similarity. Literally draw a line from one side of the T-chart to the other, trying to link up similarities. Here's an example of my connections.

PASSION   EXPERIENCE

Passion	Experience
Personal Development	Sales
Beach	Mom
Babies	Worked for Zig Ziglar
Like-minded people / Seminars	Dancer
Pugs	Author / Speaker
Faith	Leadership Roles
Making a Difference	Moved a lot as a Child

Where do you see a connection? If you do this right, you will likely see MANY connections and MANY possible book ideas. If you have more than one, the easiest way to pick your first book topic is to ask: Which one of those topics speaks to me the most? Which would be easiest for me to write? Which will help me leverage my authority?

The reason that passion and experience, and the intersection of the two, are so critical is because without one or the other, your book project is doomed to fail. If you write a book about something you are passionate about but have no experience in, your book will lack depth or credibility. If you write a book about something in which you have experience but no passion for, you will not have the motivation to finish the book. It has to be an intersection between the two in order to write a book that a reader wants to READ and one that you WANT to write.

Now that you have your topic, let's move on to Rule # 3.

Rule # 3 – DO NOT wait … Start writing

The third rule of writing is really the hardest. I see it happen over and over and over again. Most would-be authors and leading authorities fail because they do not follow through with rule number three: start writing.

This is so hard because there can be many distractions and limitations keeping you from writing. Your calendar is not going to automatically open up and give you an extra ten hours a week to write. So you have to find the time to do it. There may be other things that could potentially hold you back, too. I often see people who have a great topic and are excited to write a book get stuck because they experience doubt or fear, or they lack the support from friends and family to keep them going.

That is part of the reason I wrote this book. To help you stay on track. Once you know that you have a topic that can make a difference and help somebody personally or professionally, you need to get that message out into the world. The best way to do that is with a book. You can leverage your book and build it into your authority platform. There is no reason to let fear, distractions, or procrastination hold you back.

Questions for Clarity

Now that you have identified your possible book topic, here are a couple of questions to help you get clarity on what you are trying to accomplish with this book and help you to get it "out of your head and onto paper."

- **What is your book's subject?** *(Ex. Leadership, business, personal development, real estate, etc.)*

  _____

  _____

  _____

  _____

- **What is it about?** *(Ex. How to be more productive, how to sell a business, how to find the right dentist in your area, etc.)*

  _____

  _____

  _____

  _____

- **What is its purpose?** *(Ex. Inspire, educate, persuade, etc.)*

  _____

  _____

  _____

  _____

- **What do you hope to accomplish?** (Ex. Build your authority, make a difference, get more clients, etc.)

  _____

  _____

  _____

  _____

- **Why does your book need to be written?** (I'll give you a hint ... you have a story and your story matters.)

  _____

  _____

  _____

  _____

- **Where is the market for your book?** (Ex. Business owners, nurses, women, parents, etc.)

  _____

  _____

  _____

  _____

Now that you have more clarity about the topic of your book and its audience, we are going to get all your ideas onto paper.

Mind Mapping Your Book

Once you know your topic, you are ready to begin mind mapping your book. This effective technique—one that I did not invent but I use to map out my books and our authors' books—will help you to get all those thoughts running around in your head out onto paper. Since 2010, I have done this exercise countless times at my "Book Bound" workshop, and I have yet to have a single person fail to get their entire book mapped out, start to finish, chapter by chapter, sub-chapter by sub-chapter, and stories within the chapters. So, let's use this process for your book, too.

If we were doing this exercise in person together, I would give you a large piece of flipchart paper and some markers, and I would tell you to find a big plot of carpet, wall, or somewhere that you can spread out to get creative. But you can do this where you are now with any size sheet of paper and a few colored pens, pencils, or markers, and you will get the same effect. The key is to commit to doing this without distraction, so for the next hour, put away your phone, your laptop, and anything else that could get in the way of you completing this exercise.

If you give yourself the time, you will get the results you are looking for. This is your time, so do not waste it. Often, I see people fail because they have great ideas to put into a book to become the authority in their field, but they just do not do it. Do not let that happen to you. Do not waste this time. Get out your paper, and let's go.

> Ask yourself, "What is everything I know about this subject?" This is the first step to mind mapping your book.

Once you have your paper and your markers, ask yourself, *"What is everything I know about this subject?"* This is the first step to mind mapping your book. Mind mapping has been around a long time, but I happen to use it for writing books. It is one of the best tools I have ever discovered to get everything that is going on in your head out onto paper. First, draw a circle in the center of a piece of paper and put the core message there. This is the main topic of your book.

Then, draw six to eight lines leading out from that center circle, and list everything you know about your subject at a very high level. For example, when I was writing my book *Winning in Life Now – How to Breakthrough to a Happier You*, I sat down and thought "Okay, what is everything I know about being a winner in life? What would I want to share with my sons or my family about what I have learned to 'break through to a happier you?'" Immediately I thought, "I would want to tell them about the importance of thoughts and beliefs. I would talk about gratitude, balance, self-worth, etc." So I listed each of these things as high-level components stemming out of the center circle.

The key here is to write whatever comes to mind. Be sure to stay focused on one area until you have everything out of your head and onto paper. Then do the same thing for each individual circle. So I did the same thing for self-worth, beliefs, and balance. Be sure to stay on each area until you have thought of everything you can and then move on to the next idea.

Once you have covered all the different main points, go back and think through the stories, examples, case studies, and testimonials that you can use to support your points. Begin to think through any other material you can add to that topic to create more flavor and substance in each one of those sections. It is as simple as listing key words that will trigger stories or ideas that you can use in the actual writing process. Remember, you are not writing full sentences yet. You are literally just writing down key words as placeholders, knowing you will come back to those stories and points later.

For those that do not have the time or desire to do this exercise on your own, we will work with you and do this exercise for you in-person at your office or ours. In just a couple of hours, we will literally pull your entire book "out of your head and onto paper" and provide you with an entire book outline. If you would like our team to work with you one-on-one to expedite this process for you, email us at Support@ThePowerofAuthority.com to schedule a consultation.

Once this process is complete, you will have the structural basis of an outline for your book. At this point, many authors take that outline and post it on the wall where they can see it every day. When they have ten or twenty minutes of free time, they can pick a topic from their outline and start writing about it.

Ways to Become an Author Without Writing

If you are like many people for whom writing does not come naturally, or those that do not have the time or inclination to sit down at a computer and write for hours on end, then there are other ways to write a book without actually writing at all. Simply, grab a voice recorder or pick up your smartphone. There are plenty of apps that you can use to record yourself talking about your topic. Then you can have that recording transcribed, and that becomes the basis for your chapters.

If you really do not want to write or you do not think you have the time, there are other resources available, such as working with a ghostwriter or collaborative writer who can interview you and create your book for you. You still get the credit as the author, and you have final say on editing. But this is a great way to get your book done quickly and one of the more common ways we help our authors get their books done fast.

There are multiple ways to go about it. Just find the easiest way for you to get your ideas out of your head, and then begin mapping your thoughts out onto paper. There is no right or wrong way, so pick the way that works best for you.

How to Get Other People to Write Your Book for You

I am not talking about ghostwriting here. Instead, these are methods that you can use to leverage other people's experiences and knowledge for your own book. One strategy is to publish a book of case studies that highlight your clients' or patients' success stories. You can interview them or record them telling their stories, and then transcribe it to be edited for your book. For example, if you are a chiropractor, you could highlight how you have helped people with different neck injuries, lower back pain, or hip pain. If you are a financial planner, you could have chapters on retirement planning, long-term care, and wealth transfer. Each section would tell the story of one of your clients or patients, and point readers to the benefits you provide.

Another way to get other people to write your book for you is to interview people. This is essentially what Napoleon Hill did with his classic book *Think and Grow Rich*. A more modern example would be Tim Ferriss' book *Tribe of Mentors*. In it, each chapter is organized around certain topics, and it basically is an edited transcript of his podcast's interviews with guests. You could also record and transcribe a panel discussion or a keynote speech that you have given and have an editor modify it to read in book format.

You Are the Expert of Your Own Story

By following the passion and experience exercise and by mind mapping your book, you will have a complete book outline and the confidence of knowing what you should be working on at any given point in time. Again, this is the exact process I have used for all of my books, and we use this process for every one of our authors that publish with us. It works time and time again.

Never forget, you are the expert of your own story. You already have the passion and experience. Now it is all about getting your thoughts onto paper.

"You can make anything by writing."

— C.S. Lewis

CHAPTER 7

HOW TO PUBLISH
YOUR BOOK

Now that you have your book mapped out, let's talk about what comes next: the publishing process. Knowing what your book is about and having a plan for starting to write is one thing, but now you need to start thinking about how you are going to get your book into the hands of the people that need to read it most. You ask, *"Okay, how do I do that?"* Well, the answer is you do it with publishing.

The Six Steps to Successful Publishing

There are six steps in the publishing process, and I will cover all of them for you in this chapter. As I said earlier, writing a book is like following a recipe. You just need to follow the proper steps in the right order, and you will be well on your way to enjoying the success of being an author and growing your business. Publishing a book can take time if you do it on your own, but the good news is there are ways to expedite this process with a little help. Whether you navigate your own journey to authorship or fast track it with a publishing partner like Performance Publishing Group, the six steps in the publishing process remain the same.

Step # 1 - Prewriting

Prewriting is everything that you do to gather and organize your ideas. This is the part of the process where you find your topic, identify your target market, and brainstorm the message you want to share with your clients and patients. Prewriting would also include the "Finding Your Topic" T-chart exercise and completing the mind map. If you have followed the steps that I have shared in this book, you should be ready for the next step in the publishing process.

Step # 2 - Drafting

Drafting is when you get the first draft of your book "out of your head and onto paper." You can type it on a keyboard, or you can write it out with a pen and paper, if you like. The majority of busy professional authors speed up the writing process by recording themselves talking about their books, chapter by chapter. You could also have a writer interview you and write the entire book for you, which is what we do frequently with our publishing clients.

In this drafting stage, it is important that you do not worry about your mistakes or typos. Do not write a sentence or two, and then go back and reread it for editing because that will totally stop your train of thought and flow of creativity. Your first draft will never be your final manuscript. This step is about getting your thoughts on paper in what I call a "brain dump." Your first draft will have lots of typos, and there will be mistakes. At this stage, you are just trying to get those ideas down on paper. Edits and corrections will come later.

> **Your first draft will never be your final manuscript.**

Step # 3 - Revising or Proofreading

The third step in the publishing process is revising or proofreading your first draft by going back and refining your writing. Review your notes and ideas, and check them for clarity and completeness of thought. Make sure that you told your story the way you want it to be told. This is not full on editing yet, but rather it is making sure you are expressing your thoughts clearly and accurately.

With revising or proofreading, you are trying to make sure things read smoothly and that you are getting your point across. To do this, you may have to read and reread your first draft many times. It is not necessarily a fun part, but it is necessary if you want to have a book that reads well. Since nobody knows your story like you do, you will have to be the one to proof it before an editor gets involved, which leads us to the next step in the publishing process.

Step # 4 - Editing

There are many different levels of editing, and I do not want to get too far into the weeds here because this is the kind of stuff that most busy professionals prefer to let someone else handle, like we do for our publishing clients. But, it is important to point out because it is a critical step in the publishing process.

Editing can be a simple editorial analysis, or full on ghost writing. The level you need will be determined by your writing ability, style, and budget. Most authors look for someone to *copy edit* their book. At this level, an editor is looking for typos, spelling errors, and run-on sentences. They will ensure that your book reads well and flows appropriately, which is very important.

Should you need a little more help, there are editors that focus on *book doctoring* or *heavy editing*. In this case, an author needs help with the basics of copy editing and the actual writing. These editors spend a lot of time revising or rewriting what an author has already written, to ensure it reads well.

The highest level of editing is what we call *ghostwriting* or *collaborative writing*, where a writer and an editor assist you with your writing. For example, there are many people who have a great story to tell, but they just do not have the ability to write it out very well or the time to do it. A ghostwriter helps you get your book out of your head and onto paper through an interview where they ask you questions, get out all your best ideas, and then write the book for you. A ghostwriter is typically unknown, meaning their name is not associated with your book. You are listed as the author. In actuality, this is how most books are done these days.

Step # 5 - Design

There are two types of design involved with publishing a book—the interior design and the exterior design. Interior design, otherwise called formatting, is done after editing is complete. This process will make your manuscript *look* great, whereas editing makes your manuscript *read* great. During this process,

> Formatting will make your manuscript look great; editing makes your manuscript read great.

your paragraphs are formatted correctly, graphics are included, and the layout is finalized. In this stage, you can add quotes in call out boxes or add images.

The exterior design is your cover design. Your cover design can be completed at any point in the process once you have finalized your title. The front and back covers are designed with photos, your title, and book description. The designer will create a whole look and feel for your book. All of this is done prior to your book going on to the final step in the publishing process.

Step # 6 - Publishing

The final step in the publishing process is the publishing or printing of your book. There are several publishing options available to you, which I will describe in this chapter, and you must make additional decisions regarding the type of book you want to publish. Will it be a physical book or an eBook? Do you want it to be a hardback or paperback? There are many decisions you will need to make at this stage. The most important decision is which publishing method will be right for you and who will help you in the process.

Three Publishing Methods

There are three main publishing methods available to you. I will discuss the pros and cons of each so that you can make the best decision based on your needs and desires.

1. Self-Publishing

Self-publishing is the cheapest route to take, but it can also take the most time. It does require a great deal of effort and involvement on your part. You will need to be well-versed in the process to ensure that you are following all publishing guidelines and that you are producing a quality book, but it is doable.

However, this tends to be the least desirable approach for busy professionals because it takes so much time, and time is money. For those that do not have a lot of extra time to learn and execute a new process, I recommend the second method, which is what I call partner publishing.

2. Partner Publishing

There are pros and cons with each of these publishing models, but partner publishing has more pros than cons. By outsourcing the work involved to produce your book, you have found the fastest path to getting your book published. Partner publishers have the resources and the ability to get your book through the publishing process professionally and quickly. Of course, with anything you outsource, you are going to pay more than if you did it yourself, but if your name is going to be on a book, wouldn't you rather pay a little more to have it done right?

> **Partner publishers handle everything for you.**

Partner publishers handle everything for you. This eliminates the need to spend hours, weeks, or months getting in the weeds, trying to find and hire editors, designers, and printers, and navigating the book registration and distribution process. Bottom line, if you are writing a book to build your authority, strengthen your brand, get more clients, and leverage what you already know, then partner publishing is the best route for you.

The best part of partner publishing is that you retain 100% of the profits, and you also retain the full rights to your book. That is very different from working with a traditional publisher.

3. Traditional Publishing

Traditional publishing is what most people think of when they think of publishing—you know, the large publishing houses in New York City with all the famous authors getting paid in advance for writing their books. Yes, that is fantastic, but it is not the reality for most first-time authors, especially if you are writing a non-fiction book.

The traditional publisher will do all of the work for you which sounds nice at first, but you will have no control over the publishing process. You literally hand your manuscript over to them and then trust that they will produce the book in the best possible way. They will pick the design. They will edit your stories. They will choose where to distribute it. Worst of all, they will own 100% of the rights to your book. That means they own your story as part of their intellectual property. In addition, they also take approximately 80% to 90% of the profits from your book sales. That is huge! And, even though they own all the rights and take all the profits, *you* still have to do all the marketing. That's right, when you work with a traditional publisher, they do all the work of producing your book, but you actually have to do all the work of marketing it and generating sales.

So unless you are a huge celebrity or already have a massive global brand, it is going to be very, very hard to market and sell your book at a national or even international level. If you have to do all the marketing anyway, why not just partner publish and keep all the profit? That way you can keep all the rights to your book, have full control over the publishing process, and get the book out into the hands of the people that need it most.

If you are planning on using a book to build your own authority platform and grow your business, then traditional publishing may not be the best route for you. Just remember these pros and cons as you consider your book publishing decision. You can keep the rights of your book and all the profits when you partner publish or self-publish, which is very important for new authors.

Performance Publishing Group

Our company, Performance Publishing Group, is a partner publisher. This means that we will do all the work for you to get your book out of your head and into the hands of the people that need it most, and we do it through online distribution. You keep 100% of your profits and 100% of your intellectual property rights. We have published authors from all sorts of backgrounds and professions.

> We will do all the work for you to get your book out of your head and into the hands of the people that need it most.

Partner publishing and done-for-you publishing services are in great demand by busy professionals because nobody has the time to stop what they are doing, put their business on hold, and take the time to learn the process of writing, publishing, and marketing their book. It is just too complicated and time consuming. That is why so many professionals and service providers have chosen Performance Publishing Group as their partner publishing solution. Just take a look at what some of our clients have had to say about our process:

"As a CEO running a company and trying to write a book, **I did not have time to figure things out. Michelle took the burden off me so I could focus**. She brought in an A-team of professionals in each critical success area to help me get this project done. **Michelle is amazing with her wisdom and advice.** The end result was a book that surpassed my expectations. **I could not have come close to this finished product on my own."**

— Dave Larson,
CEO Sales & Marketing Technologies

"I just got back from the post office and shipped out more copies of my book Content First Marketing. **This book was the result of an effort that was actually quite painless.** Michelle Prince took me through the process. We started with a collection of different documents that I had written, and we wrote those into a manuscript. That manuscript was the foundation for this book. And then she took me through the editorial process and getting images. She guided me through this so that I was able to have a published book at the end. **Her done-for-you publishing services make it even easier because she gets it done for you**. If you are looking for someone who can help you with your book and you know that you have a book within you to propel your business forward, **I strongly recommend Performance Publishing Group."**

— John Arnott,
CEO Clear Again Media

"The communication between me and the team was seamless and professional. **I would highly recommend Performance Publishing Group."**

— David Kauffman,
Empowering Small Business

*"Michelle's guidance throughout the process **made it easy to get started!"***

— Bob All,
Owner of Customer Security Specialists

So that is why we do what we do—to help people like you get their books done right and done quickly. That way, you can get it into the hands of the people who need it most and use it to grow your business right away.

The Benefits of Being an Author – No Matter the Book Size

Did you know that the benefits of becoming a published author are available to you no matter the size of the book you write? That's right! These benefits—credibility, notoriety, and leveraged opportunities—all come to you whether you write a full-length book, a chapter in a book compilation, or a "business card"/mini-book. In fact, mini-books can be a very profitable marketing tool and work well in practically all professions. It is something that I use myself, and I have seen significant results.

> Mini-books can be a very profitable marketing tool and work well in practically all professions.

Here is how it works. Whenever I am with a prospect, speaking at a conference, or attending a networking event where there is a potential opportunity for me to help someone, I will give them my "business card" that happens to be a mini-book called *Your Book is Your Business Card.* That one little book, used as my business card, has brought in more opportunities than I could have ever imagined. It is only 5,000 words, which is not much, but it has blown away any other marketing approach I have ever done. I have seen it work time and time again because people will throw away a business card, but they will not throw away a book. It is also more affordable than writing and publishing a full-length book due to its size.

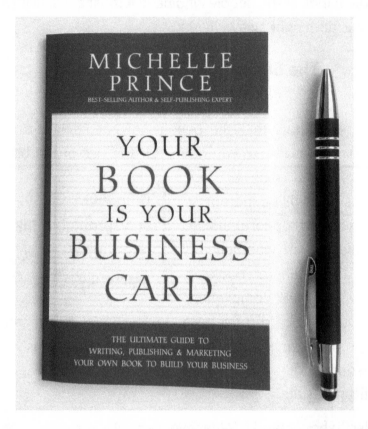

There is a huge benefit in both mini-books and full-length books because they serve different purposes. Many of our publishing clients use their mini-book as their business card, which is their "lead magnet," and then they use the full-length book to sell in their practice, at conferences, or to give to clients or prospects to gain that credibility factor.

I recently heard a great story about this. One of my new clients told me that I gave her my "business card"/mini-book over a year ago. It had been sitting there on her desk ever since because she said she could not throw it away. So every day when she saw my book on her desk, she thought of me and my partner publishing company. Finally, she said, "I need to do this," and so now we are publishing her book. That is the power of being an author! And that is the reason behind my writing this book. You can experience *The Power of Authority* and use it to grow your business, whether you write a full-length book, a mini-book, or a chapter in a book collaboration. Your authority as an author is the same.

"You are the same today as you'll be in five years except for two things, the people you meet and the books you read."

— Charles "Tremendous" Jones

CHAPTER 8

BECOME THE AUTHORITY TODAY

I hope you have enjoyed this journey because you are now well on your way to turning your dreams into reality. In these pages, I have given you all the tools you need to become THE leading authority in your field, grow your business, and create more opportunities as an author.

Your authority will automatically attract new and qualified prospects who seek you out for the products and services you provide. It will also allow you to charge a higher premium and elevate your status. Being an authority gives you more significant positioning in the marketplace. It all but eliminates the competition. Becoming an authority by authoring a book will give you the additional revenue, respect, and results that you deserve.

> **Becoming an authority by authoring a book will give you the additional revenue, respect, and results that you deserve.**

Think about this:

- *What would it be like if you never had to make another cold call again?*
- *What would the exposure of being seen and heard on top media outlets do for your business?*
- *How would a 10-20% increase in profitability affect you and your family?*

Just imagine all the benefits of being an author that are immediately available to you when you publish a book. You will have:

- An effective way to overcome price resistance with prospects
- More opportunities for speaking, coaching, and consulting
- A system for automatically generating new leads
- Additional revenue streams for your business
- Constant requests for media appearances
- Expert positioning in the marketplace

All of this is just waiting for you when you author a book.

Become the Authority Today

If you have been following along with the exercises, then you have identified your topic, mind mapped your outline, and considered which publishing option is right for you. The last step is actually getting your book finished, and that is where I can help. If you are ready to take the next step, then I invite you to email us at Support@ThePowerofAuthority.com to schedule your free, no-obligation 30-minute call to discuss how we can help you get your book done quickly, effortlessly, and in the hands of the people who need it most.

Becoming a published author can do more to exponentially grow your business—over the next year, five years, and the rest of your lifetime—than anything else I know. If you want to be THE leading authority, then you have to write a book. It has never been easier to get your book done and done right, but you need to take action before your competition does it first. Remember, there can only be ONE leading authority in your field, and YOU should be it.

> **If you want to be THE leading authority, then you have to write a book.**

I encourage you to master the skills in this book and claim the authority that you deserve. Really decide once and for all that you are going to leverage *what you already know* to increase your revenue, get more results, and help more people. I hope you will make the decision to take action and leverage **The Power of Authority** in your business by becoming an author today.

ABOUT THE AUTHOR

Michelle Prince is a best-selling author, sought-after motivational speaker, CEO and founder of Performance Publishing Group, a "partner" publishing company dedicated to making a difference ... one story at a time. She's helped thousands of professionals around the world become published authors through her consulting, courses, seminars, and done-for-you publishing services. She is the founder of the *Book Bound Workshop* (www.BookBoundWorkshop.com), which helps soon-to-be authors get their story "out of their head and onto paper." Michelle knows we all have a story, and she is passionate about helping others tell their stories so they can make an impact in other people's lives. Michelle is also an enthusiastic, dynamic speaker who captivates audiences with her authenticity, high energy, and natural ability to connect with any audience. She has been endorsed by some of the most influential speakers in personal development, including Zig Ziglar, and she currently serves as the "Ziglar Brand Ambassador," representing the values and legacy of the late Zig Ziglar. Michelle has been married to her husband Chris for 22 years, and she has two teenage sons, Austin and Tyler. They live in McKinney, Texas. Learn more at www.MichellePrince.com

PERFORMANCE
PUBLISHING GROUP™

MAKING A DIFFERENCE... ONE STORY AT A TIME

ABOUT PERFORMANCE PUBLISHING GROUP

Performance Publishing Group provides top quality, compre-hensive book publishing services for soon-to-be authors. Led by best-selling author, Michelle Prince, the Performance Publishing team has helped hundreds of people realize their dream of becoming an author. As a partner publisher, we can offer you more than just expert guidance, we want to make sure you get the book of your dreams and reap the rewards. Years ago, we saw the opportunity for a better publishing process, so we created it. We know how tricky it can be to write, publish, and market a book, and that's why we'll be there for you every step of the way.

We've jumped the hurdles so you don't have to! Tap into our decades of experience, and see how easy it can be to share your story. We've crafted a solid method that will help get your story out of your head, assist you in writing your book, and have the publishing and marketing resources to support and move you closer towards your goal.

We have various resources apart from our done-for-you publishing services, such as book consulting, digital courses and live events. If you think one of these options is more your speed, let us know! We want to find a plan that works best for you.

www.PerformancePublishingGroup.com

972-529-9743 x 106

Support@PerformancePublishingGroup.com

CPSIA information can be obtained
at www.ICGtesting.com
Printed in the USA
FSHW010123031019
62554FS